P9-DUJ-165

YELLOWJACKETS

Smart apple   15.95   8-22-95

YELLOWJACKETS

Text and Photographs by

EDWARD S. ROSS

THE CHILD'S WORLD

I'm a yellowjacket. You have probably seen me before. I like to eat off of your plate at picnics and may try to steal tidbits from your school lunch. If you bother me, I sting!

There are many different species of yellowjackets. We are a kind of wasp. As you might guess from our name, most of us have yellow-and-black jackets, but some of my relatives are black and white or orange and black.

Like ants and honeybees, yellowjackets are social insects. We live in large nests, some containing hundreds or even thousands of wasps. All of the wasps in a nest are produced by one female, called a *queen.*

This is how my mother looked last winter. She was hibernating under the bark of a tree, with her wings, legs, and antennae tucked up against her body. She was too cold to move, so she had to hide from her enemies. She lived off the fat stored inside her body.

When spring arrived, the weather warmed enough so that my mother could fly. She found a sheltered place and started to build a nest. It was called a *queen nest* because she had no offspring yet and had to do all the work herself. First she flew to a tree and chewed off tiny pieces of bark, just as this wasp is doing. She mixed the bark with her saliva to make paper.

Yellowjacket nests are made entirely of paper. This is why we are often called *paper-wasps*. The paper we make is similar to the paper in this book, but rougher and not white. We were the world's first paper-makers. In fact, humans got the idea of making paper from chewed-up wood by watching us make our nests.

My mother started her nest by attaching a paper stem, which looked something like the stem of an apple, to a tree branch. Then she added about twenty small compartments, called *brood cells*, with their openings face down. She made the middle cells first and laid eggs in them. The eggs hatched, and grublike baby yellow-jackets, called *larvae,* gradually developed. Each larva hung upside down, its tail end glued to the cell by a sticky secretion. To protect the brood cells, my mother enclosed the cluster in two layers of paper. The whole nest was a little larger than a golf ball.

My mother not only made the queen nest all by herself, she also collected food for her first-born larvae. Soon these larvae were full grown and stopped eating. Then each larva, using glands in its mouth, spun a white silk cover over its cell. Each closed cell was much like a moth's cocoon. Inside, the larva transformed into a *pupa*. At first each pupa was white, but gradually it darkened as the colors of the developing adult wasp showed through the pupa's thin skin.

This photograph shows every stage of our development—cells containing eggs, others with growing larvae, and some silk-covered cells containing pupae. Some of the covered cells have been chewed open by adult wasps that have already emerged.

Toward late spring and early summer, when temperatures rise and food is easier to find, the number of adult wasps in a nest steadily increases. At first, all of the wasps in a nest are sisters who are unable to reproduce. We are called *workers*—for good reason! Each morning, as soon as it is warm enough to fly, most of us go out to find food or wood fibers to enlarge the nest. Some of us stay in the nest and feed the larvae, or stand guard at the nest entrance, ready to fly out and sting an enemy.

With all of us helping, my mother can really act like a queen! She no longer has to help build the nest or look for food. All she has to do is lay eggs in the new cells we build. My sisters and I even feed her, passing food from our mouths into hers.

Mature yellowjackets eat liquid food obtained from many things. Our favorite is the juice of a chewed-up insect, especially a caterpillar. We also like the juices of dead animal meat, plant sap, and flower nectar. In this photograph, we are eating a rotting apple—fallen fruits are another of our favorite foods. Especially on hot days, you can see us drinking water from dripping faucets or mud puddles.

As larvae, we were fed these same liquids, but also accepted tiny bits of solid food. My adult sisters and I enjoy feeding the larvae in our nest. We look like mother birds feeding their young! When we tickle a larva's mouth, it spits up a sweet fluid droplet. Some scientists think that the only reason we bother to feed the larvae is to get this sweet treat.

Late in the summer, when the nest is really thriving, some of my mother's larvae develop into future queen wasps—females that hibernate through the winter, build queen nests in the spring, and then lay eggs. A few other larvae grow into males. We do not get to know these brothers very well because they leave the nest soon after they become adults. They live only a short time—just long enough to mate with the future queens, as shown in this photograph.

We workers make space for our growing family by making plenty of new paper. We chew up tiny pieces of wood, mixing it with saliva to make a ball of sticky pulp. Then we fly back to our nest, holding the pulp in our jaws. Hanging upside down and moving backwards, we flatten the pulp along the edge of the paper enclosing the nest. Each streak in the paper represents one flattened ball of pulp. We also carry balls of pulp inside the nest to make more cells. As the nest grows, we chew up the inner layers of paper and use the pulp to enlarge the nest even more. We wasps were recycling paper long before humans did!

If we live in a city where there aren't many trees, we gnaw fibers off old buildings and other wood surfaces—even painted ones! The paint adds color to our nest, as shown by the colorful streaks in this photograph.

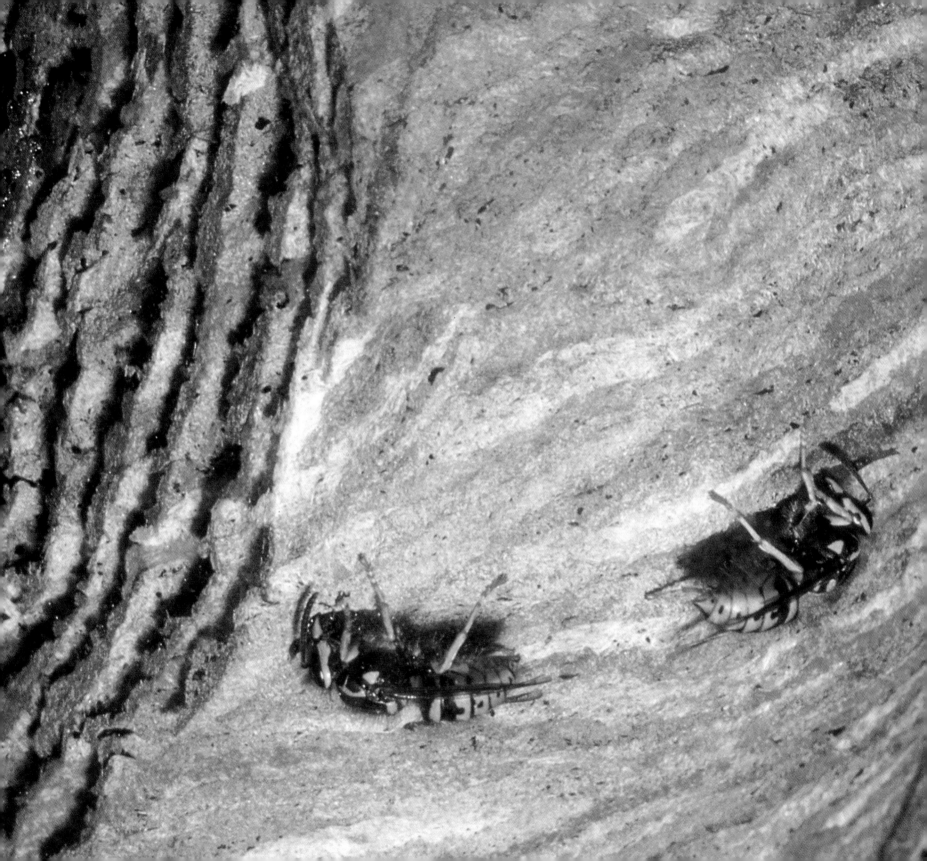

All social insects make nests to hold their young—young that our enemies know are juicy and good to eat! The nests of honeybees also contain stored honey, which many animals love to eat. To protect all of this, social wasps and bees often build their nests in high places, out of the reach of bears, foxes, and other potential robbers. They also protect their nests with guards. If something disturbs the nest or gets too close, guards at the entrance signal the other insects to stop whatever they're doing and attack the enemy.

In the world of wasps and bees, only females can sting. A honeybee's stinger stays in her victim, so she can sting only once. But a yellowjacket's stinger can be used again and again.

⇐ *Long-horned Beetle*

⇑ *Clearwing Moth*

⇐ *Flower Fly*

Because many animals like to eat insects, we protect ourselves by flying away and, if we are caught, by stinging. Young animals learn what is safe to eat by experimenting. If they get stung, they remember—just as humans would—never to bother anything that looks like the creature that stung them! Our bright yellow-and-black bands are very easy to remember.

Many other, less common wasps and bees look very much like us yellowjackets, so our enemies avoid them, too. Some harmless, good-tasting insects also look and act—or even buzz—just like yellowjackets. By mimicking us, they too avoid predators that would otherwise eat them!

Although we can defend ourselves against enemies, we have a difficult time with cold weather. You could have walked right up to the nest in this photograph. The picture was taken in early winter, and the yellowjackets that once lived in the nest have died from cold and lack of food. The future queens that grew up in the nest have flown away and are hibernating under tree bark or in other sheltered places. During the winter, the wind blows apart most nests, but this one is still in good shape. In this cut-open nest, you can see five levels of cells where baby yellowjackets developed the summer before.

We have many paper-making relatives, especially in warm, tropical regions. Some types of yellowjackets build their nests underground—usually using a hole dug by a small animal. Our most common relatives, called *Polistes wasps*, are shown in this photograph. Like us, they live in both warm and cool climates. Polistes wasps do not cover their nests with a paper shell. Instead, they hang their nests in protected places, such as under bridges, broad leaves, and the eaves of houses. Some Polistes wasps are bad tempered and fly out and sting people who get too close.

Most people think that yellowjackets and our relatives are mean, annoying insects, but actually we are an important part of nature! Because we kill caterpillars and other insects, we help control pests in gardens and on farms.

If we happen to build a nest near your house, don't walk up to it or throw stones at it! We don't like to be bothered, and will chase after you and sting. Instead, stand quietly a safe distance away and watch us leave the nest and return with food or paper pulp. If you move slowly near our nest, we might get used to seeing you and not bother you at all. After all, we don't usually bother humans unless they bother us!

INDEX

Text Copyright © 1993 by The Child's World, Inc.
All rights reserved. No part of this book may be reproduced
or utilized in any form or by any means without written
permission from the publisher.
Printed in the United States of America.

Library of Congress Cataloging-in-Publication Data
Ross, Edward Shearman, 1915-
Yellowjackets / by Edward S. Ross.
p. cm.
Summary: Describes the development and daily activities
of yellowjackets from a worker's point of view.
ISBN 1-56766-017-7
1. Yellow jackets (Insects)--Juvenile literature.
[1. Yellow jackets (Insects).]   I. Title.
QL568.V5R67   1993   92-42934
595.79'9--dc20   CIP
                                                          AC

Distributed to schools and libraries in the United States by
ENCYCLOPAEDIA BRITANNICA EDUCATIONAL CORP.
310 South Michigan Avenue
Chicago, Illinois 60604